DISCARD

The *Dirt* on
Drugs

Justin Lookadoo

Revell
Grand Rapids, Michigan

Hungry Planet

© 2005 by Hungry Planet

Published by Fleming H. Revell
a division of Baker Publishing Group
P.O. Box 6287, Grand Rapids, MI 49516-6287

Printed in the United States of America

Library of Congress Cataloging-in-Publication Data is on file at the Library of Congress, Washington, D.C.

ISBN 0-8007-5919-2

Published in association with Yates & Yates, LLP, Literary Agents, Orange, California.

Interior design by Brian Brunsting

What's Inside

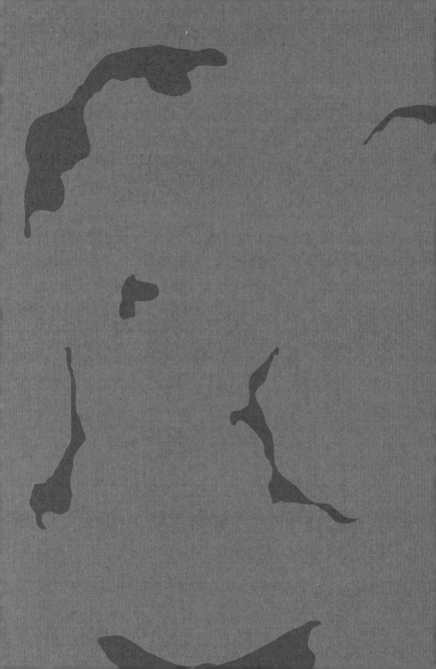

the dirt

GETTING STARTED

I have a question for you: What do you want to do with your life? What kind of stuff do you want to experience? To have? Places you want to go? This is our starting place. Don't leave here. Let's get a picture of your life.

(Mr. Book Designer, hook us up with some space to write.) If you need more than this go get your own paper. We'll wait for ya.

Let's do some dreaming and get it inked on paper. What's your dream? What do you want to do? "I don't know" is not an answer. This stuff can change, but right now, today, what do you really want to do? Scribe it. If you're a short-answer person, make a list. If you're a writer person, then write it all out in a story. Scribe with your vibe.

Cool. Now where do you want to go? Skiing? Paris? Scuba diving? Europe? What? Write as many places or things that you would totally love to get into.

Oh, and what stuff do you want to have? What kind of car? Where do you want to live? House? Apartment? Beach?

What's your life like? College? Graduate school? Family? Kids? Just think about your perfect life.

Now check this out. The average life span of a person is about 83. Here's a little something for the visual learners like me:

Born   **83**

How old are you now? Don't know? Then go ask your momma. Put an X where your age fits on the line.

Now think about when you hit 70. What kind of 70-year-old do you want to be? Do you wanna be that hip oldie-but-goodie cruising around in the convertible chasing all the hot 60-year-olds, dancing and play-ing all night?

Or do you wanna be that grumpy old person sitting in some lonely nursing home having some nurse feed you Jell-O and fiber while you sit around with the other old people waiting for the highlight of the day . . . *Wheel of Fortune*? I mean, think about it! Really think about it. Hey, if you're not going to play, then stop reading and go away. This is important stuff. You have to think about your future so you can plan your now.

Let's shift gears here and do a little imagination thing. Some of you are sitting there saying "Do we have to?" The answer: "Yes," said in an overbearing, grumpy-old-man voice.

This is going to help all this drug stuff make sense. I promise . . . sorta.

Okay, when I give you an age, you shut your eyes for a brief sec and imagine what your life will be like at that age. K? Think about who you are, what you are doing, what you have, and what you have accomplished. Where have you gone and what have you done? Just let your mind run.

Let's go to it. Imagine all of this stuff when you are . . . 25. What do you look like? Are you fat and outta shape? Are you healthy and feel good? Did you graduate college? Where are you living at 25? I'm sure you've met some new friends. What are they like? What do you guys like to do together? Are you married? If so, what is your honey like? If not, who are you dating? Shut your eyes and build that life in your head. Make it the life you want. And again, if you're a writer, feel free to scribble it down. When you finish check back with me. Now go.

Stop reading. Go and get your life in your head. I'm not writing another word till you do it. Okay, I have to write, but I'm doing it under protest until you do it.

Now, how 'bout 35? What's your life like at 35? Jobs, trips, places you have gone since you were 25? Married? Kids? House? How much are you making? Go through your mental movie time. Go.

Do a big jump to 60 years old. A 25-year leap. Now what is life like? Where do you live now? Kids? Grandkids? Do you play with them? What have you done in the last 25 years? Where have you gone? Box seats at the Super Bowl? A month in Paris? What's life like? Go.

Man, that's pretty exciting stuff, eh? If yours wasn't that exciting, then go back and do it again, and this time *make* it exciting. Here's the beautiful part about life: You do get to plan it. You get to make the choices now that will start getting you closer to your goals in life. Now this wasn't a full-on "how to design your life" program; that's a different book. This was just more of a little compass thing to get you going in the right direction.

You gotta hang on to all this stuff while we are talking drugs. Keep it in your mentals, 'cause sometimes it's hard to see a lot of bad stuff about drugs when you are just living in the moment. But your life is way more than just a moment. That one blip in the DVD of your life could affect the rest of your world. I mean, obviously stuff like crack and heroin has major short-term effects. But with stuff like tobacco, alcohol, ecstasy, and marijuana, you have to look past today and do a little looking into your future to see the major downers. So remember, your life isn't short-term. You're gonna have to deal with all the stuff you do today. You can't just focus in on this little section of your life and think that's all there is and nothing more. That would be like going to a movie, watching the first 10 minutes, and then leaving. Just because you didn't see the rest of the movie doesn't mean it stopped. The flick kept rolling. And just because you choose not to look at your future doesn't mean that the decisions you make today won't change your life tomorrow. They will. So as we do the whole drug thing . . . uh . . . I mean, discuss drugs intelligently, keep focused on the fact that your life is about more than just today.

drug menu

Alcohol
The Battle of the Booze

Quick Q: How old do you have to be to get alcohol? No, wait, bad question, 'cuz in some places it's pretty easy at any age. So how about this: how old are you *supposed* to be? Yeah, the big 21. (I know that in different countries the ages are different. So just insert the correct legal age for your land and keep reading.) Another question: Why 21? What's so magical about this number? What's your guess? And no, "I dunno" is not a guess. Use your hat rack and think about it. Is it because that's when you are considered an adult? Well, no, that can't be it. Here in the U.S. you are considered an adult at 18. So is it just some random number the old men in the government

alcohol

cocaine

ecstasy

ghb

inhalants

marijuana

oxy

ritalin

steroids

tobacco

picked? Uh . . . that doesn't sound right. How 'bout something simple?

Let's get all biological for a sec. The shell you're walking around in called the human body takes time to cook. Just because you popped outta your mamma doesn't mean you're done. Now, everyone used to think that your brain was totally developed by the time you hit your teen years. But the brain scientist people have found out that the brain keeps on developing until somewhere between 21 and 24 years old . . . hmm, there's that 21 number again. Are you sniffing the jelly yet? Are you catching the connection between 21 and alcohol? If not, we shall continue. If so, please keep reading. Yeah, either way, keep going.

I want you to understand something here: I am not anti-alcohol. This isn't one of those "if you drink it you're going to hell" sessions. If you are on the opposite end of the booze battle and are totally anti-alcohol, that's cool. There is nothing in the Bible that is anti-alcohol, but it is anti-drunk. Absorb that into your men-
tals. I am not hatin' on you
or your fam if they drink.
And I'm not punkin' them
if they don't. But I am saying that if you want to do
it, hold off till you're at least
21. Stick with me and we'll
get to the whys.

Let's dig deeper into the brain thing. Bio 101: the brain is the most important thing you've got. It controls everything. Walking. Talking. Learning. Even the stuff you don't see like the blood flowing in your veins. Your nose running. When you have gas. Everything. Now, this mushy, Spam-looking lump of stuff is über-sensitive to alcohol. And alcohol totally changes the way the brain does things. Plus, since alcohol is a depressant kind of drug, it slows down the pace of the brain's functioning. Now, when you enter this world, about 40% of your brain wiring is connected. That means there's about 60% waiting to get plugged in. So all through the kid times, through the teen years, and up to around 21, the brain is still working on the wiring. It is making the connections that need to be made and cutting out the connections it doesn't need anymore, making the brain run faster, smoother, and without as many glitches. It's kinda like getting computer programs synced up to run better.

In the body, alcohol has an all-access pass. It can get into any place in the brain. It's like a computer virus that totally interferes with the brain's communication system. Instead of getting the right messages for development, it's like talking on a cell phone with a crappy connection. But

alcohol

cocaine

ecstasy

ghb

inhalants

marijuana

oxy

ritalin

steroids

tobacco

instead of saying "What?" over and over, the brain just makes any connection possible, even if it's wrong. That's why they say that people who start their heavy drinking as teenagers are stuck in adolescence. It's because their brains didn't get wired right and that changes the way the brain is supposed to work.

Dude, think about that. Stuck in adolescence. **How would you like to spend your entire life stuck in 8th grade?** Oophta! No thanks.

Use your little image-maker in your head and you can visualize the way the brain starts getting wired wrong. But for those of you who are list people, here is a little something for you—a list of the brain stuff that alcohol affects.

> **learning**
> **remembering facts**
> **reasoning**
> **language**
> **problem solving**
> **movement**
> **mathematics**
> **grammar**
> **spelling**
> **identifying objects**

Those of you who like quotes from expert people, this is for you: According to the people at Alcohol Healthwatch,

"Studies suggest that adolescent brain development involving memory, language skills, problem solving and attention is adversely affected by alcohol."*

Are you catching it? The brain has to finish the setup. Alcohol gets in the way and changes the way the brain gets wired. All of this stuff is the major reason for the age 21. That's when the brain is usually finished developing.

Then we've got the total body issue. Again, it's about giving the body time to get the system flowing the way it's supposed to. It's not a question of alcohol being good or bad; it's a question of timing. Check it. If you saw a baby who just started walking, would you jet him off to the gym, crank up the treadmill full speed, and throw him on it? Oh, but no! He'd shoot off and hit the wall like a ping-pong ball. (No babies were harmed during the writing of this statement.)

Why wouldn't you do it? Obvious Guy says, "Uh, 'cuz he's not ready for it." Yeppers, that's it. His body hasn't

*http://www.ahw.co.nz/alcohol_health_promotion.html

developed enough to handle that yet. Does that mean treadmills are bad? No matter what your overweight aunt says, the answer is no, treadmills are not bad. It's not about the treadmill. And it's not about the alcohol. It's about body development. You gotta give the bod time to finish growing before you start adding things that could tear it down.

Here are some other things that get messed up by alcohol, especially when they haven't even fully developed yet (yeah, and that means until around 21). Again, this is for the list people reading the book:

liver – that's what has to process all the alcohol so it won't kill you. And too much alcohol can shut the liver down.

lungs – no, it's not like smoking, but alcohol can siphon out some of the important chemicals the lungs need to work right.

pancreas – okay, you don't have to know what the pancreas does; just know that you need it and alcohol could jack it up. (For those of you who simply must know, the pancreas makes enzymes and hormones like insulin.)

While You Were Out

What do you think of when I say *teens*? That's right, hormones. (Okay, I don't think of that either, but let's continue.) The whole teen experience is crazy anyway, from beginning to end. It starts with growing hair in places you don't want to see. Zits start popping out and looking at people. You hate the way you look, your voice sounds like a dying owl, and you are happy, sad, depressed, excited, weak, and all-powerful. And that's just while you're brushing your teeth. What's happening is that your brain is signaling all these hormones to dump into your body at just the right moment in order to develop you into, well, you. It seems like your brain and emotions have just gone crazy and kinda checked out. But listen, while you were checked out, your hormones were totally remolding your brain and body.

Throw alcohol into this hormonal soup and things really get weird. Check it. Being a teen is hard enough as it is, right? Pretty stressful stuff. Put alcohol in your body and it kicks up the corticosterone a few notches. That may mean nothing to you now, but it will. This stuff is a stress

cocaine ecstasy ghb inhalants marijuana oxy ritalin steroids tobacco

hormone. So here's the process. Life freaks out and gets stressful. You drink a little alcohol to ease some of the stress. The stress is relieved a little. But the stress hormone is amped up because of the alcohol. See how this could go bad fast? You end up on this merry-go-round of stress, and you can't seem to jump off.

Girls, for you, big-time drinking can cause the problems that you already know about, but it could also give you pain with your period and, if you get pregnant, either a spontaneous abortion or a baby with major birth defects.

For the guys we'll take it back to sex, of course. Fellas, long-term drinking is connected to your business not standing at attention, your little swimmers not swimming, and your jewels shrinking. All because alcohol was thrown into the mix while the hormones were trying to do their job.

What else about alcohol? Oh, this: teens tend to drink more than adults, and it's kinda by accident. See, for some reason teens don't feel the effects of alcohol as easily as adults do. Like the whole slurred speech and stumbling around stuff. And since they don't feel like they are wasted, they risk drinking more, which makes them an even bigger target for puking, passing out, getting alcohol brain damage, and even dying. Again, it's a body development issue.

Booze Does the Body Good?

Everyone is latching on to this study that said drinking alcohol reduces the chance of heart disease. I have looked at all the info I could find, so I'll break this down the best I can.

First of all, they are talking about adults whose body construction is complete. (I know this is getting really, really, really, *really* repetitive, but the whole body-brain development thing trumps all other research.) In fact, they have done most of their studies about alcohol and health on really old people.

Now, they have found that drinking red wine seems to make people less likely to die from one form of heart disease. I do not doubt this. Several studies are showing the same thing. But here's the problem. They didn't take into consideration the total lifestyle of the person. I mean, if you wanna fight heart disease, put down the six-pack and the fried chicken and try walking to the corner and picking up a salad. They really can't say that it was definitely the wine reducing the risk. So when you are ready to make your own decision to drink or not, don't base it on keeping you healthy. That's not the right answer.

alcohol
cocaine
ecstasy
ghb
inhalants
marijuana
oxy
ritalin
steroids
tobacco

Healthy Drinking

The National Institute on Alcohol Abuse and Alcoholism said this about the health benefits of drinking alcohol:

"In the elderly, moderate drinking has been reported to stimulate appetite, promote regular bowel function, and improve mood."

So if you're an anorexic, depressed granny with irregular poop cycles, drink up!

Why Oh Why?

Why do people drink? Peer pressure? Stress? Advertising? Yeah, all of these are pieces of the puzzle, but the bottom line is the effect. Yeah, alcohol makes people feel more relaxed, so they have less social hang-ups and they feel free to have fun. But there is a fine line between having lower anxiety and sleeping with some dude at a party.

A fine line between feeling free to have fun and smashing your car into a minivan full of kids.

Bunches o' people claim they need alcohol to loosen them up to have a good time. Actually, I think they just need an excuse to have fun. Check it. When I was in college there was a special recipe for party punch called Grandma's Hot Toddy. Whenever there was a throwdown, GHT was sure to be there. Well, a friend and I decided to do a little experiment. We threw a party, and we made Grandma's Hot Toddy. In fact, when people showed up to get their party on, there were still empty liquor bottles all over the kitchen. People came, they drank, they got stupid! I wish we would have taken pictures, 'cuz it was crazy. Oh yeah, and one more little detail—there was no booze in the Toddy. Not a drop. We grabbed a bunch of empties from other people's trash and threw them around the kitchen. We poured a little on the floor so there was definitely the smell there. We mixed up the GHT like it was normally made, minus the alcohol. Then we just sat back and watched. It was the funniest thing ever. People did things that they would never normally do but needed an excuse to do. They just needed an excuse to get stupid.

Listen, if you wanna get crazy, do it. You don't need alcohol, drugs, or anything else. All you need is permission. Well, here ya go, I give you permission. So if you want to sing for no reason, dance in the middle of the coffee shop, laugh out loud, climb to the top of a tree and act like a monkey, whatever, I give you permission. Let it be known that you have official permission to get loud, be obnoxious, scream, talk to people you normally wouldn't. Whatever you want to do, I give you permission to do it. And now when you decide to get crazy, you have an excuse. Just tell them, "Lookadoo said I could."

Sober Up!

If someone is totally wasted, there is nothing you can do to get them sober. Coffee, cold showers, exercise, nothing. Yeah, you can pump a lot of coffee into someone, but all you will get is a wide awake drunk who has to pee a lot. They will still be drunk. The body has to process the alcohol, and you can't change that.

Alcohol
Makes Me Loose
I mean "Loosens Me Up!"

So what happens when you drink? Here's a little role play. Say you don't want to feel weird at a party where everyone else is drinking, plus you think that if you drink you'll feel a little looser and more relaxed. You'll be not so uptight so you are able to laugh with your buds and chat up the hottie.

Now add some of the other stuff that we have already talked about like the fact that teens drink more 'cause they don't show the drunk-signs as quickly as adults do. So you have several drinks 'cause they don't really seem to be affecting you. And hey, it makes you even *more* relaxed.

Well, since you didn't realize you were drunk until it was too late, you ended up yelling at your best friend, dancing on the tables to some '70s disco, and puking all over the hottie. Then you just kinda lost track of what happened, but from what you hear, you hooked up with someone you barely know. And now you have this burning going on down there, and you have to show your face at school on Monday where everyone knows what you did . . . well . . . everyone except you.

You don't think it will happen to you? This stuff happens to millions of teens just like you who swore they would never do stuff like that either.

Check it. Teens who use alcohol and other drugs are 5 times more likely to have sex.

More than half of sexually active teens say that drugs and alcohol influenced their sexual decision.

Sixteen % of teens who drink use condoms less often after drinking, and those who do use them probably don't use them right so they lose their effectiveness anyway. I mean, they can't pronounce the "th" sound, so what makes you think they can put on a condom?

Guys, if a girl is drunk, high, stoned, or anything else, DO NOT do anything sexual with her. [Note to the Naïve: I am not condoning any sexual activity outside of marriage. But, hypothetically speaking, if we happened to live in another world besides the perfect one some of you seem to think we live in, this stuff needs to be said.] No matter how much they might say they want to or how much you want to, don't do it. In fact, you and your boys need to keep each other in check on this one. 'Cause if you do have sex while she's messed up, you can get tagged for rape. It doesn't matter if you happen to be drunk too. You're still getting busted. I know, it's not really fair, but that's the way the system works right now.

Girls, do not put yourself in a situation where you can be taken advantage of. Understand that if you get wasted, some guys are going to take advantage of that.

Here's the tricky part, people. When both of you are tore down, neither of you win. Trouble comes especially when people have sex while they are wasted and they really hadn't planned on it. Guys, you'd better hear this and believe it. The courts just set an unbelievable precedent on this. A girl snuck out of the house, went to a party, got drunk, and hooked up with some dude. They had sex, she was caught by the parentals, she accused him of rape, and now he's in jail for a crazy amount of time! I don't know what really went on, and I am not blaming anyone here. But all this could have been prevented.

Girls, if you get pregnant or even think you might be, DO NOT drink any alcohol. Listen, maybe you've made up your mind about how you are going to handle the pregnancy or maybe you haven't, but no matter what, do not drink. This is feeding the baby straight alcohol. It will cause all kinds of birth defects. Even if you give the baby up for adoption, you will have to live with the guilt that you purposely chose to do something that totally deformed and ruined another human's life.

All right. We have had quite a little discussion about alcohol. Let me just throw it out there one more time before we say goodnight: I am not for or against drinking. All I want you to do is wait. Give your body time to develop the way it's supposed to. And who knows, you may discover you don't wanna touch the stuff at all.

cocaine

ecstasy

ghb

inhalants

marijuana

oxy

ritalin

steroids

tobacco

Cocaine. It doesn't matter if we are talking about white powder or little rocks of crack; it's still cocaine. The diff is in the way it is processed. Cocaine is processed with ether, so it's a little more risky—ya know, dopers working with explosive materials . . . not good. Crack is processed with ammonia or baking soda and water to form hard rocks. It's processed differently, it's used differently, and it costs different amounts, but it's all cocaine.

The stuff has a few other differences, though. Crack is a purer, more concentrated form than just powder cocaine. And it gets into the body a lot faster than the snorted stuff. That made me wonder, *Why would anyone use powder cocaine?* I mean, it's way more expensive and gives a less intense immediate high. So why not go straight for the crack?

A lot of people on cocaine think they are going crazy.

Before we get to that, let's look at the pay-off. You've heard a lot of horror stories about coke and crack, but there's gotta be some kind of payoff or people wouldn't do it. Well, there is. Cocaine gives you this warm feeling that all is good. It gives you this brain jolt so it's like your mentals are firing strong. You just feel like you are *it*. Unstoppable. Beautiful. Powerful. You are the package.

When snorting coke, the peak hits in about 20 or 30 minutes and then starts to fade. With crack, the time is a lot shorter. And that is part of the answer to why some people do powder instead of crack. See, a crack user just hits this zone of being king of the world and it starts fading fast. That's when people start upping the hits and doing more, and then they cross the line of having to get their next hit no matter what the cost. They will do anything.

The beautiful-feeling coke moment is quickly replaced with paranoia. You think everything is wrong. Everyone is out to get you. You become your own mood ring, quickly changing from one mood to the next. And it totally messes up your brain. A lot of people on cocaine think they are going crazy. They know something is wrong; they just can't figure out what it is. What they don't

cocaine

ecstasy

ghb

inhalants

marijuana

oxy

ritalin

steroids

tobacco

realize is they have lost their memory, their ability to pay attention or remember conversations, and even their ability to process what is happening. In fact, someone has to tell them that cocaine has totally changed the way their brain works. Oddly enough, some people feel better when a doctor tells them they have brain damage from coke, because at least they know they're not going crazy.

But go back to the question, *Why would people use powder over crack?* Check it. Believe it or not, there is a status thing in the drug world. Crack is for dirty, worthless junkies. Cocaine is for the well-off and well-to-do. They would never lower themselves to do crack. That is so beneath them. Man, you don't know how many former crack addicts I have talked to who started with that same attitude. But it doesn't take long to cross that line to doing crack. It's a weird social dynamic thing, but it's real.

Bottom line: *any* form of cocaine will get in your head and mess with the feel-good chemicals in your brain. This is where the high comes from. The problem is that when you start messing with brain processes, you don't know how it will turn out. But it's never a good thing. So if you wanna feel good, let your body handle it. Working out, running, riding roller coasters—these are some healthy ways to get the feel-good chemicals flowing. This gives you more power and more control over how you feel, and you stay in control of what you do.

Double Trouble

Mixing cocaine and alcohol is extremely dangerous. Yeah, first is the danger of 2 drugs floating in your bod, but it gets even more scary. See, the human liver does this little voodoo trick that combines cocaine and alcohol and manufactures a totally new and different substance called cocaethylene. This intensifies everything about the drugs. The highs, the negatives, and even the risk of sudden death all skyrocket. So a note to the high: if you are stupid enough to do cocaine, don't magnify your stupidity by chasing it down with booze.

Double

Mixing cocaine and
dangerous. Yeah, f
2 drugs floating in
even more scary. S
does this little vood
cocaine and alcoho
totally new and diff
cocaethylene. This
about the drugs. T
negatives, and eve
death all skyrocket
If you are stupid en
don't magnify your
booze.

ecstasy

ecstasy

ghb

inhalants

marijuana

oxy

ritalin

steroids

tobacco

Ecstasy is the fad of the moment in the drug world. Drugs have fashion cycles just like clothes. And right now, X is it in the drug culture.

But now this is starting to change, partly because of the huge attention it's getting. Just like fashion, when 30 people all have the same shirt, it's no longer a cool thing.

It's the fashion cycle.

Someone wears it and it catches a little attention.

Then a lot of people jump into it, and now it's overdone.

The fashion dies.

Except for a few die-hard fans who will be stuck with that dorky haircut forever because they don't want to let go of that fashion. Another reason is that people are starting to figure out that X isn't some cute little party drug with no downside. People are getting seriously messed up.

Let's look at the whole ecstasy scene. I'll state the obvious for you (actually this is for the adults who are sneaking a peek at this book): most ecstasy is not used in the rave and underground party scene. But that's what adults think because a few years ago raves became a hot news topic and the media targeted ecstasy use at the blowouts. Now, don't get me wrong; ecstasy is used at these places, but it's more of an anywhere, anytime kinda drug. Hey, think about where you have heard about people doing the stuff. Yeah, some of it has been at the all-night parties, but most of the time it was someplace else. A friend's house, going out on the town, a movie, whatever.

People are getting seriously messed up!

ecstasy

ghb

inhalants

marijuana

oxy

ritalin

steroids

tobacco

Repetitive Qualifying Statement:

Not every drug affects every person the same way.

Besides just media hype and the cool factor, there have to be reasons for the ecstasy overload. And like always, there are some goods that go along with X. [**R.Q.S.**] These are just some of the things that could happen. With X comes an extreme good mood vibe. It's like all is right with the world. If you do it you may drop the walls you usually put up. That kinda softens your ego so you don't worry what other people think and you are more open. You get all these warm feelings of love and empathy. Your senses seem to kick into hyperdrive. Light, sounds, and touch are intensified so your body is super-sensitive to this stuff. You have an urge to connect with people, to touch them, to kiss them. Basically, ecstasy magnifies the human desire to experience people more deeply. And sure, if that was all that happened, it'd be great. But ecstasy opens up a lot more things we have to look at.

Touchy, Touchy

With ecstasy your sensation of being touched can become **intense**. Being tagged with the desire to touch other people and connect with them on a deeper level puts you in a situation of doing and saying some really stupid things. Tons of people have sexed it up with someone and in the moment felt it was so right. But when they come down, they hit that wall of "uh-oh." Pregnancy, disease, guilt, just feeling stupid . . . all of those thoughts flow right in and smack you into reality. I even heard about one dude who took X and made out with another guy. Problem was, the dude on X wasn't even gay. You talk about dealing with some issues.

Is Your Secret Safe?

You don't even have to have sex with someone to really get weirded out by this "freedom" you found with X. Some people just totally connect and tell each other everything. All their secrets, dreams, past. They pledge undying love for each other. Then they come down and are looking at this person they just told all their deepest secrets and promised to love forever—and they may not like or even know the person.

Peace, Love, and T.M.I.

Okay, would the world be a better place if we were a little more loving? Yes. But some of our walls are there for a reason. They are there to protect us. Anything that totally destroys those walls could totally destroy our lives. If you let just anyone behind those barriers, you have given them access to your deepest core. You have given them control of your life, your emotions, the real you. This is great with someone you know and trust, but it can crush you when it's with someone you are just getting stoned with.

One of the weird things with ecstasy is that it seems to **disable the body's ability to regulate temperature**. This makes me laugh, in a sick and twisted way, when I think about X being used at some all-night rave. You have people who are dancing their butts off with no ability to regulate temperature. Yeah, nothing bad can go wrong here . . . That's why one of the biggie causes of death at these parties is overheating. There may be lots of fluids and energy drinks being slammed, but this doesn't help. In fact, it makes the X even more dangerous. Your body needs to shut down and get cooled off. But the energy drinks keep people out on the dance floor where they just keep pushing the body temp up until they blow a fuse.

So Hot

Here's another twisted little trick X plays. Ecstasy actually interferes with the body's ability to process ecstasy. So basically X goes into the body, but the body doesn't want it, so it starts trying to get it out, and the X goes, "No, I'm going to stay around for a while," and starts jacking with the removal process.

DOUBLE CROSS

This is why bumping X and taking another hit when the initial high is wearing off is so dangerous. The body hasn't been able to process the first hit before more of it gets shoved in.

Crash Test Dummy

The main prob with X is not the effects of the drug while doing it but the stupid things that people do while on it—well, that plus the crash.

After the peak of X comes a major crash, and this is where things can go bad yet again. If the Xer makes it through the roll without doing something that will physically or emotionally trash them out, they still have to deal with coming down. Many people feel totally drained the day after. In fact, some people just blow off the day after 'cause they feel so bad. Man, talk about throwing your life away. I mean, literally, the next day is a trash day, and they know it ahead of time. They are given another day to experience what this life has to offer and live it to the fullest, and many users just totally waste it. Then after they get back to life, many go through an after-X depression that could last the entire week. A few users will continue to experience the depression for weeks after.

Besides the depression stuff, you could get a whole variety pack of downers like irritability, being moody (even more than usual), crying for no reason, not being able to focus or get anything done, having your eyes weird out on you, and having problems remembering crazy simple stuff like your phone number.

...depression that could last a week

Now remember, we are not talking about hard-core dope fiends here. We are talking about regular people like you and me who also (unlike me!) hit some X on the weekend.

Short-term stuff ain't the only issue either. There's some long-term stuff that you probably don't want.

ecstasy

ghb

inha

arijuana

oxy

ritalin

steroids

tobacco

Brain Rewire

No one knows for sure what's happening to the brain or what damage is really going on, but here's the latest info. The expert scientifical-type people say that X damages the axons in the brain. Axons are kinda like cables that have to be plugged together to send messages to make your body work. Ecstasy messes up these axons. Now, the supporters of ecstasy say, "Yeah, but the axons grow back." Well, yeah, technically they do. But the regrowth is not normal. They don't grow back the way they were. It would be like if you got your arm cut off and your body grew another one straight out your back. Sure, you still have 2 arms, but you have to change everything you do—the way you live, work, and play—and your clothes won't even fit. That's what happens to the brain. It gets rewired, and no one really knows what the effect of this will be because they haven't studied it long enough.

I have a friend who took X back in the day when it was still legal. He told me that if we could get pure ecstasy, he would love for all his friends to take it together. Ahhh, and there lies the problem—**there is no such thing as pure X anymore.** Even if you take it to one of those little portable wannabe drug labs set up at raves to test the "purity" of the stuff for you, they are basically just testing to see if there is actually MDMA (ecstasy) in the pill. But check it: most X in today's scene is only 40% pure. So guess what? Sixty % is mystery meat. Stuff thrown in to make more pills out of less product. That's why it's such a huge risk. There is no such thing as real ecstasy anymore.

The bottom line of X is that in its pure form . . . well, we can't discuss that 'cause there's no such thing anymore.

So the real bottom line is that there's lots of stuff out there called ecstasy that has some level of MDMA in it. But you can't really predict what will happen when a person takes it because of the 60% unknown stuff in the tabs.

As for the personal connection you feel, if you wanna explore the side of you that longs to connect with living creatures, don't jump into the middle of the ocean without a life jacket by taking X. Instead, get a pet. A dog, a hamster, a fish even. That way if things go bad, it won't be as hard to fix. Hey, it's a lot easier to flush Nemo down the toilet than it is to repair your life from the damage done by ecstasy.

ghb

inhalants

marijuana

oxy

ritalin

steroids

tobacco

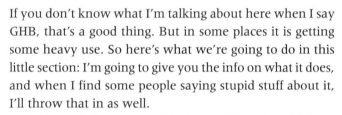

If you don't know what I'm talking about here when I say GHB, that's a good thing. But in some places it is getting some heavy use. So here's what we're going to do in this little section: I'm going to give you the info on what it does, and when I find some people saying stupid stuff about it, I'll throw that in as well.

GHB stands for **Gamma Hydroxy Butyrate**, which really means nothing to me, but know that it is a weird and unique drug. It seems to combine the effects of several drugs all together. You get the effects of ecstasy, alcohol, steroids, and sleeping pills all wrapped up in one little thing. GHB starts out in a powder form, but not very many people ever see it that way 'cause by the time it hits the street it is dissolved in liquid. So for the most part it is swallowed like any other drink—well, except for the addition of a dangerous chemical.

XEffect

Lots of times GHB is used at clubs kinda like ecstasy. In fact, one of the little pet names is Liquid X. It seems to have some of the same effects, like the whole feeling the music vibe, getting that desire to connect with others, and losing a lot of those inhibitions that are there to protect you. Pretty much X kinda stuff. (Check the Ecstasy section for more details.)

Alcohol-Free Drunk

When a little more GHB is used, it snaps into almost an alcohol feel. Drowsiness, slurred speech, the whole drunk feel. Using even more of it shoots you straight to puking and losing consciousness.

Some researchers have said that there seems to be some promise in this drug to help alcoholics get off the booze. This would probably be a good time for me to throw out a well-known fact about GHB: it is addictive. People seem to have to up the dose to get the same effect, and then when they don't get the drug, they go through withdrawals.

I'm not a doctor of, well, anything, but it seems to me that if you are trying to get someone off alcohol by giving

ghb

inhalants marijuana

oxy

ritalin

steroids

tobacco

them another chemical that has the same effect as alcohol, is addictive, and makes your body build up a tolerance so you have to have more, then you have just made them an alcohol-free drunk. Sure, they're not an alcoholic anymore, but now they're a junkie. Hmmm . . . makes you wonder.

Sleep Tight

Many people say that GHB is a great sleep aid. Well, sure, anything that knocks you out is a "great sleep aid." Here's a prob I have with the rationalization of this statement. I was on a research-based website—ya know, people who should *not* be idiots—and on it John Morgenthaler and Dan Joy reported that "small doses produce relaxation, tranquility and drowsiness which make it extremely easy to fall asleep naturally."* Okay, I guess I don't understand the definition of falling asleep *naturally*. To me, falling asleep naturally means WITHOUT DRUGS! C'mon, man, that's like saying that a plane allows humans to fly naturally or that a 30-year smoker died of natural causes. It just doesn't make sense.

Now let me throw this at ya: the people who are all for GHB agree that to use it safely, you have to follow the dosage exactly. Any small increase in the dose could turn

* http://www.erowid.org/chemicals/ghb/ghb_faq.shtml

things real bad, real fast. Well, actual GHB is in powder form. You can measure it and gauge it. But it is mixed into a liquid before it is sold to the user, so you can't measure how much you get. This is why the emergency rooms are getting lots of biz—because there's a very fine line between sleep aid and coma aid. And you can't see that line in liquid form.

PUMP IT UP!

GHB has been getting play in the bodybuilding world because it seems to increase the production of human growth hormones. So some people are using it as an alternative to steroids. Which might sound like a good idea until you throw in all the other little things like the addiction, the coma, and the drunken stupor. Great, you have a bigger body and a stupider brain.

Warning

GHB has been put in the same group with Rohypnol as a rape drug. Just like roofies, it has been linked to lots of sexual assaults.

I can't believe what I just found on the same site as the other "medical" info on GHB. Listen to this. They are boasting about the sexual benefits of the drug. They call them "prosexual benefits." Here's what they said:

45

> Perhaps the foremost prosexual property of GHB is disinhibition. Some users suggest that GHB's other sexual benefits are secondary effects, made possible (or at least amplified) by this loosening of psychosomatic constraint. A number of people have commented that this disinhibition is particularly marked among women. *

Okay, I'm a little ticked off right now, so I'm going to try to be as polite and professional as possible without telling you what I really think about these . . . grrrrr . . . idiots. Let me break this down to you very simply. Remember, we are talking about a drug used in sexual assaults! And these fools are promoting it as good. "Perhaps the foremost prosexual property of GHB is disinhibition." What that means is that the drug will drop all your natural defenses that you have to protect yourself. It puts you in a position where just about anything seems okay in that moment. You don't worry about consequences or tomorrow. They also said,

* http://www.erowid.org/chemicals/ghb/ghb_faq.shtml

"Some users suggest that GHB's other sexual benefits are secondary effects, made possible (or at least amplified) by this loosening of psychosomatic constraint." Understand what "loosening of psychosomatic constraint" means. That means you lose the ability to say no. To stop yourself. To rationalize and connect right and wrong. You just go along with whatever is happening. Are you connecting how rape comes into play? Now crown it with the final statement, "A number of people have commented that this disinhibition is particularly marked among women." Listen, these people are telling sexual predators or just stupid lonely jerks out there that women are easier targets when you slip 'em GHB. And they are saying this as if they are giving you scientific findings. It makes me want to rip their heads off.

Listen, GHB is bad news. It is totally messing people up and destroying the lives of many girls who have had to live through an assault because someone gave them some GHB. Stay away from it. Girls, make sure to protect yourself (check out www.safety.can/ articles/keep-an-eye-on-your-soda.html). Meanwhile, I gotta go for a walk 'cuz I'm so mad about this stuff.

inhalants

If you haven't noticed already, most drugs give some kind of payoff that gets people to start doing them. Even some little teeny tiny little thing that is positive can be why people get into them. Well, for inhalants it's not really that way. I mean, yeah, they are way cheap and easy to get. So is toilet water, but I'm not running to a public restroom with a straw and some Kool-Aid.

Let's start at the beginning of the huffing maze. You know what inhalants are, right? Anything with fumes that people sniff. Simple stuff like permanent markers, gas, white out, butane, spray paint, fingernail polish, even the gas that comes out of whipped cream cans. Anything that has some fumes that people sniff.

When someone takes any of that stuff and sniffs or huffs it through the nose or mouth, it quickly shoots straight to the brain. The immediate effect makes you look, from the externals, kinda like a drunk. It's an initial rush of "whoa" and then drowsiness, lightheadedness, and even the whole passing out and puking stuff. Get clear here—this is the "good" stuff that comes with inhalants. All of this happens so fast that you have to take another quick hit to get the buzz back. When the inhalant is bumped up with another hit, then you redline into the danger zone. The old stuff is still in the body, and the organs kick into overdrive, fighting like crazy to process the crap. When the second flow shoots through, it is total overload and hyper-dangerous because of the high concentration of the body-destroying chemicals in the body. Okay, that's pretty much the good stuff. Yeah, I know, not too glam, but that's all I could really come up with.

Now let's hit some of the negatories. How about death? I'm not just talking about a couple of people falling out every few years. I am talking about enough deaths that it's now its own syndrome. No, I'm not making this up. It's called Sudden Sniffing Death Syndrome. Their heart is beatin' along just fine, they sniff an inhalant, and

OST DRUGS GIVE SOME KIND OF PAYOFF . . .

. . . FOR INHALANTS IT'S NOT REALLY THAT WAY.

BLAM

their heart blows. And this could happen with just 1 hit. In fact, 22% of people who died this way were first-time users.*

But that's not all. The hits just keep on coming with the whole death thing. There's the possibility of dying because of asphyxiation, which is just a cool way of saying, "You ain't got no O_2 in your lungs." Oh, and then there is the fun of suffocation, which happens a lot when people fill a bag full of something to sniff and then put it over their heads. Don't they read the labels? Plastic bags are not toys.

Here's another fun effect of sniffing fumes: brain damage. Complete and irreversible. See, the inhalant totally invades the brain and pops brain cells. You know how frustrating it is when you can't remember something? Something easy like where you left your science book? Well, imagine that is your life. Only you can't remember stuff even a kindergarten kid should know, like your phone number,

22% OF PEOPLE KILLED BY INHALANTS WERE FIRST TIME USERS

* http://www.intheknowzone.com/inhalants/stats.htm

your birthday, even how to tie your shoes. You know you should know this stuff, but you just can't. And it doesn't ever get better.

Then we kick into all the organ damage. Lungs. Liver. Kidneys. Inhalants could shut 'em all down.

I even remember reading in the paper about this really intelligent dude who was sniffing propane and decided he wanted a cigarette. I think they called the cause of death "stupidity."

A major reason people are getting really **messed up** with inhalants **is** because **they** look around and **compare themselves with** their **friends**. They think, "Look, all these other people are doing inhalants and not falling over dead or getting their brains fried." So they just get it in their heads that what I am telling them is flat-out wrong.

Well, I hope you understand this before it's too late: I'm not wrong. But a couple of things could be happening here. First, inhalants don't affect everybody the same way, and they don't even affect the same person the same way every time. Second, maybe you are not noticing how stupid your friends are getting because you are getting as stupid as they are. Don't get sucked into believing that just because inhalants are not illegal and are easy to get they must not be bad.

Marijuana time. I thought this was going to be a really huge section with lots of cool info and stuff. Man, I have researched, I have read, I have looked, and I have figured out that this is the most studied drug and one that has produced more meaningless crap in the name of science than any I have ever seen. So I am going to give you what I have found and my take on the world of marijuana and just leave it at that.

First let me throw this out there: if you do anything, smoke anything, drink, even burp because you feel scared or weird because other people are doing it and you are not, you need to snap outta wuss mode and make your own decisions. Check it. If you really don't wanna do something other people are trying to get you to do, then just

Teens who smoke MJ are 4 times more likely to get pregnant or to get someone pregnant.

tell 'em no. If you feel that way, I guarantee others feel that way too. You take the out and you'll probably have people hit the exit with you. And even if you end up solo, you'll feel a lot better and a lot stronger by not doing it than doing it. Comprende?

The main effect that you hear about on TV or see in the movies is that marijuana just really mellows you out. Okay, yeah, that is one effect. But again, like with most drugs, there are lots of things that play into this. If you are in the middle of a fight with your parentals, it probably

will not mellow you out. In fact, a lot of people get freaky paranoid instead. They think all their friends are talking about them or that they have been left alone at a party (even though they know everyone there).

Legal Schmeagal

I love the "legalize marijuana" people. So many of them say it should be legalized because it's not as bad as alcohol.

Okay, with that intelligent argument we should legalize shooting you in the foot because it's not as bad as shooting you in the face. Pretty stupid, eh? Just because something is not as bad as something else doesn't mean either one should be legal.

Really, Officer, It's Prescription

Does marijuana have medicinal uses? Well, yes and no. Smoking dope doesn't have true medicinal use. The stuff that's helping people is a couple of chemicals in the MJ. One is THC and the other is cannabidiol (CBD). Researchers are finding that these two things help in many medical cases.

So what they are doing is finding out a way to get the THC and CBD into the body without granny taking a bong hit with all her homegirls down at the recreation center, yo! What they have come up with so far is a THC pill, but they're working on a more effective mouth spray.* You just spray it in your mouth and there ya go. It's not totally ready in the U.S. yet, so people needing the THC and the CBD are having to find other ways to get it. Some are still arguing that it's easier to control dosage and effect and works better when you smoke it. Awww, poopie. They just wanna smoke dope. With the different strengths of MJ mixed and all the other toxic chemicals mixed in it when you smoke it, it's not the most effective way. But give the scientist people some time, they will find it.

[Ad·dic·tion] Major arguments are going on over whether MJ is addictive. Actually, that's not even the real question. They are actually arguing about what the word *addiction* really means. MJ lovers can say there's no such thing as marijuana addiction because they have such a narrow definition. See, they say that you have to have major reactions from stopping in order to be addicted. Then you have the extreme MJ haters that have this super-broad definition of marijuana addiction—that if you have ever felt like smoking a joint, you have some deep addiction issues.

Okay, I can see where both groups are coming from, and they both have lots of research to back up their points.

marijuana

oxy

ritalin

steroids

tobacco

I'm not a big research guy; I pretty much just look around and see what's happening in the real world. It's easy. I just started googling for "marijuana anonymous." I figured if there were addiction issues, there would be MA. Sure enough, there is. I hit 'em to see if they actually have members. Yep. Do they have people who had trouble getting off MJ? Yep number 2. Do they have people who worked their system and are clean? Yep the 3rd. Well, guess what . . . it's addictive.

This is where the argument pops up of "Well, that's not a physical addiction; it's mental issues." I don't care what the issue is. **If I am doing something that is controlling my life and I can't stop . . . I AM ADDICTED!** So if you're one of the people who are arguing "it's not really addiction," you should shut up and go to an MA meeting. You'll find some people who will argue with you.

Most of the dope smokers I know are idiots. But I think they were probably idiots before they started smoking dope.

MJ addicts even get slammed in the addiction community. They can't go to an AA meeting or a Cocaine Anonymous meeting 'cause a lot of times they feel stupid. They stand up and say their name and that they are a marijuana addict, and people in those meetings seem to always say, "Is that it?" Because people think it's not addictive, marijuana addicts feel stupid that they're hooked on grass instead of crack. They really don't fit anywhere. But listen, if you are one of those people, it's okay. Get to a group for MJ smokers. They will know exactly what you are feeling, and you won't even have to explain it. They'll just know.

So what have we learned here, my little dopey readers?

Number **1**, MJ makes people stupid. And maybe stupid is cool. But only if it's someone else that is stupid, not you. Number **2**, MJ is addictive and can start controlling your life. And **3**, there are medicinal uses, but they are trying to get it in a better form. And **4**, MJ is not just some little plant that is not bad for you like the media is trying to pretend. So before you start tokin', think about what is really going on. Don't buy the lies.

OXY

a subsidiary of OxyContin

If you haven't heard of Oxy, you've been living under a rock. This is the stuff Rush Limbaugh got nailed for and Jack Osbourne went to rehab for. It's been all over the media. There's not all that much to say about it though, so we are going to get to the reals and make it short and sweet.

OxyContin is the official birth name, but everyone just calls it Oxy. It's a prescription drug for pain. Not little pains like a hurt toenail but major pain like cancer. And the stuff works. It works really well. You can take a pill every 12 hours and you're solid. The tablets are time-released so they let just enough of the chemical into your bod over a long period of time.

So what's the prob? Well, number **1**, it's highly addictive. Number **2**, when you chew it or crush it, you destroy the time-release part of the drug.

Now, jump to high school or work. Someone gets an Oxy tab, and they are not needing the pain relief but are in it for the buzz. So they pop it in and chew it like a Flintstones vitamin or crush it up and snort it. What happens is that all the drug shoots into the body. Yeah, they may get a feeling of euphoria like all is well with the universe, but they may also get the stuff like headache, high blood pressure, muscle twitches, confusion, sweating, tremors, vomiting, convulsions, coma, and, oh yeah, death.

Here's a little rule to go by for our kindergarten readers:

**If it ain't yours, don't take it.
If it's time-released, don't break it.**

That's pretty much all I have to say about that.

Ritalin

Please sit down, my little hyperactive reader, and let's talk about Ritalin. Ritalin is the most overprescribed and the most stolen drug in America.* In fact, the U.S. uses 90% of the world's Ritalin, and 80% of kids on it are boys.** Listen, we are not all ADD . . . we're just boys! Stop pumping us full of drugs and let us be boys.

Okay, that gets me a little irate, but that's not what we're chatting about here. What we're talking about is the renegade, non-prescribed use of Ritalin and other drugs out there for ADD and ADHD.

* D. Machan, "An Agreeable Affliction," *Forbes*, August 12, 1996.
** http://www.drugrehabamerica.net/FAQ-ritalin.htm

Let's break it down real quick: Ritalin is speed. And I just don't get how you can give a hyperactive kid speed to calm him down—I mean, it works, but it doesn't make sense to me in my head. In fact, the human body really reacts the same to Ritalin, speed, and cocaine. Wow! That may not weird you out, but when I learned that it blew me away. The body can't tell the diff. The brain can tell a little difference though—well, sometimes.

Here's the deal. ADD and ADHD have a lot to do with dopamine levels in the brain. When the normal balance is way outta whack, then Ritalin is supposed to help balance it out. But here's the kicker: if the chemical balance is *not* off, then Ritalin acts like speed to the brain. And in an article called "Schoolyard hustlers' new drug: Ritalin," Alexandra Marks found that when abused, "Ritalin is interchangeable with amphetamine and methamphetamine, and all of them produce much of the same effect as cocaine."*

* http://csmonitor.com/cgi-bin/durableRedirect.pl?/durable/2000/10/31/fp1s4-csm.shtml

ritalin

steroids

tobacco

Trade Day

People out there are buying Ritalin and some of the other ADD drugs to take a hit so they can stay up to finish a paper or a project at work or even to cram for a test. The problem is, no one really knows what the effect of this Ritalin abuse could be because no one has studied it. It's like everyone was shocked when people started using stuff that wasn't theirs. Hellooo . . . McFly . . . I mean, c'mon, they are shipping speed into middle schools by the truckload and the world is shocked when some kids find a way to start abusing it? Who knew?

* According to Dr. Peter Breggin

This whole Ritalin thing is sneaky too. You can get hooked without even knowing what happened. You need to cram for an exam, so you just do a hit to keep your eyes open and your mind studying. It's just a study-aid kinda thing. Well, there are more tests, more projects, more things that need to get done, and hey, it worked last time, so why not? Before you know it, this little study aid is the only thing getting you through daily life. That's not a good place to be. This little pill is controlling you.

But what are the effects of this stuff?
Well, you've heard me say it before and you'll hear it over and over like a scratched CD that you have to kick to get to move on. If you are a teen abuser, the risks are way bigger because your bod isn't totally finished baking yet. Ritalin increases blood flow to the brain pretty much like cocaine does. It can mess up the growth hormones, stopping all your stuff from growing. It could cause some permanent tics, like eye twitching or head jerking, or cause depression, and could even start destroying your ability to learn.* Great, so you can stay awake to study, but your brain can't grab the info.

ritalin

steroids

tobacco

When doing the illegal Ritalin thing, a lot of people either crush and snort it or dissolve it and inject it—not smart. Yeah, this intensifies the effect, but it also destroys the time-release mechanism in the pill. Now they have an uncontrolled, unstable drug that acts like speed or cocaine, and they are shoving it into their bodies. That's why there are so many people having problems with Ritalin—because **the higher doses of speed-like chemicals become way addictive**. And since **no one really knows what it really does**, we just have to connect it to the common effects for amphetamines and coke, like high anxiety, paranoia, loss of appetite, and a whole lot more. Check out more on those effects in the cocaine chapter.

Uh . . . It's Not Mine!

Okay, it's not yours. But check it. Ritalin is a Schedule II drug. That means if you ain't supposed to have it and you do . . . you're screwed. They aren't playing on this. If you have a prescription and just share a pill or two with your friends, it could land you 5 to 20 years in the pokey and a fine of up to $1 million. If you're doing a little entrepreneurial action and selling it or trading it, the fine could jump to $5 million. Check this: if somebody dies or gets seriously hurt, it's 20 to life! And if the person injects the stuff, it blows the cap off the penalties, and they get really bad. Somebody thinks it's dangerous. Somebody thinks you're stupid for popping it if it's not yours. And that somebody could lock you up for doing it.

If you have a prescription and just share a pill or two with your friends, it could land you 5 to 20 years in the pokey and a fine of up to $1 million

ritalin

steroids

tobacco

65

GET THE BODY YOU'VE ALWAYS WANTED AND DESERVE!

THAT'S RIGHT, IF YOU WANT A BETTER BODY FAST, THEN STEROIDS MAY BE RIGHT FOR YOU.

Warning: Side effects may include aggression, mood swings, paranoid jealousy, extreme irritability, depression, delusions, impaired judgment from a feeling of invincibility, baldness, cancer, and body hair growth.

Ster

We're hearing about this steroids stuff more and more.
So let's cut through the hype and figure out the reals.

Anabolic steroids. First the good news. Yeah, they do help increase strength so you can lift more weights in the gym . . . oooh. And they do help you increase muscle mass so you look bigger . . . aaah. Well, that about covers the good stuff. Now check out some of the other great gifts that could be yours.

First, baldness. That's in the guys and girls. Both can do the whole male-pattern-baldness thing. Oh, but don't worry. Even though the hair on your head leaves, it's okay, because you'll grow it everywhere else. Yes, my little Ewok, you could be growing shag carpet all over the place.

Now for the fellas, there are some exciting gifts just for you. First of all, your testicles shrink. Yippee. This isn't some overstated anti-drug scare tactic. They really shrink! See, testicles are there to produce testosterone. If you put this fake testosterone into your bod, the testicles don't have anything to do, so they shrink down and take a vacation.

But that's not even the best part. Ya know how guys are so intrigued by breasts? Well, guys, you don't have to go looking for them any longer, 'cause more than half the fellas on these steroids end up growing female breasts. Again, not a scare tactic, a true side effect. They grow female-looking breasts.

Ladies, you too have your own personalized side effects. Yeah, you get to experience the male pattern baldness and the growing of a winter fur coat, and the facial hair is way attractive. But you also get your own breast issues. Yeah, they get to shrink. And your voice gets to get deeper. So you get a thin, ripped bod . . . but you're a dude!

Here are some things for both guys and girls: major acne on the face, back, and chest, and some long-term future risks of heart attack, stroke, liver problems, and cancer.

So do steroids have any real medical uses?

A doc can prescribe steroids for lots of different reasons. But they cannot do it specifically to increase muscle mass. And I have chatted with lots of people who say, "My grandma is on steroids, so is she going to get all buff?" Well, she may, but not because of the steroids, 'cause they are a different kind. They are probably corticosteroids and not anabolic steroids. The diff is that corticos reduce swelling and anabols increase the muscle stuff.

Here's the major question:
Do they work?

Welpers, it depends on your definition of work. If you mean do they increase muscle mass and strength, then yes. If you are wanting to increase speed, agility, and precision, then no. Here's the deal: if you are playing basketball and you can't hit a jump shot, then steroids won't help you. They will just make you a bigger guy who can't hit a shot.

steroids

tobacco

Have you ever seen one of those old pics of a body builder and then see the guy now and think, *What happened?* Well, here's the deal. A lot of times people hit the 'roids to get big quick. But they really don't have the commitment to being healthy or staying fit. They just want to appear that way. So they get big, then slack off on the working out and just keep eating. Well, all that muscle doesn't stay muscle if you don't keep using it. That's why a lot of ex-steroid users turn into the 35-year-old blob.

Obvious Statement for Clueless Readers

If you are using steroids or any other needle drug, never, NEVER use someone else's needles. No. No. No. There are so many things to go bad here. Have you heard of HIV? How about hepatitis and so many bacterial infections I can't name them all? Do not do it. Not even if you clean the needle first. NO! Think about it. He sticks the needle in him. It has all his diseases, blood, tissue, skin, and muscle cells all over it. Then if you put it in you, you just put all his body juice into you. Ugh! No way.

Most illegal steroids are made overseas and shipped to the U.S. or made in labs here in the States. Either way, don't lie to yourself and believe this stuff is made in sterile environments and regulated for safety. Uh, get real. This stuff is made in some home lab where the whole sterilization process is considered good if there are no live roaches in the recipe. Dead ones are fine.

You never know what you are actually getting. Most of the time the stuff people shoot into their body is watered down, contaminated, or just plain fake.

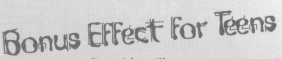

Bonus Effect for Teens

Steroids will stunt your growth.

Yeah, it sounds a little weird. Something that makes you big will stunt your growth? But it's real. Teens who use steroids run the risk of keeping it short.

You probably don't care why, but I'm going to tell you anyway. See, when you start growing, your body waits for a chemical signal to stop. The stop sign is excessive amounts of testosterone (yeah, that's in girls too). So what happens when you are in the middle of growing and you shoot a lot of testosterone (steroids) into your body is that it says, "Okay, that's enough growing," and it stops. And you're stuck in your self-induced shortness. Your bones stop growing and that's the end. This could still affect you after you get out of high school. I grew 3 inches while I was in college. So if you throw steroids into your biochemical cocktail at any time, you could shortchange yourself on your tallness.

Attention Future Inmates

Anabolic steroids are a controlled substance. That means without a doctor's prescription you can't have them, and if you do, there are things like arrest, jail, fines, strip searches and a bunch of other things you can get with your steroids.

On the Inside

I am not against being fit. I'm all for it. In fact, I am pretty obnoxious about it. But steroids get you looking like you got the fit healthy vibe going, but on the internals they're messing you up.

A lot of people get into steroids just to change the way they look. Okay, if that's you, guess what, you may see yourself looking different in the mirror, but it won't change the way you feel. So whatever issue you have—insecurity, rejection, whatever—you need to deal with that.

Now, some people who get into this stuff truly have a mental disorder called muscle dysmorphia. That means they have a way distorted view of their body. When they look in the mirror, they see themselves looking small and weak, even if they are huge and all swollen up. Even if the entire world says they're big, they don't see it.

For girls it usually plays out a little different. When they peep at their reflection they see themselves as totally fat and flab, even if they are lean and ripped. It's a mental issue. If this doesn't make sense to you, then move on, but if it does, hang with me for a sec.

Another major issue is when you've been hurt or abused. Some people get into steroids because of this stuff. In fact, a study of women weightlifters showed that a large number of women who used steroids had been raped or sexually abused.

If any of this is you, understand that these are mental issues and they need some mental fixing. Don't be ashamed of it. You're looking for a fix anyway, so you just need to look in the right spot. Get connected with a counselor or therapist or someone who can help you get your life back.

It doesn't take a CSI to see there's major evidence that people who get into steroids could go on to use other drugs—but not because they want a new high. Nope. They go on to other drugs to help deal with the side effects of steroids. Like how many of them start using opiate kinds of drugs to counteract insomnia. So then people get off steroids, but they're stuck with other addictions.

Bottom line, more than anything, steroid use is a self-esteem and insecurity issue. If you are feeling the need to get into the stuff, here's a suggestion: stop everything. I mean quit researching it. Stop planning when you are going to start. Sit down and ask yourself "Why do I want to do steroids?" You will give yourself some lame reasons at first. But keep asking yourself the question until you get a real answer. Then start working on those issues. That could be something you can do yourself, but maybe you need to find a counselor, or maybe your youth minister could hook you up with some wisdom. But if you don't deal with those issues, you will never feel the way you want the steroids to make you feel. ━

Diet Pills

I just couldn't run through all this steroid junk without thinking of the other "beauty drug"—diet pills. There are so many diet pills, powders, and drinks, it would take forever to deal with them all. So let's just be blunt and honest: for the most part, diet pills are crap. Okay, yeah, some may drop the pounds or stop the craving or whatever, but they don't work long-term. In fact, many of them do nothing for fat; they are just diuretics that make the body dump water out. It's a quick fix. And that's what we want—a quick fix. We want a pill that will get us looking good for summer beach season, but we don't want to change our lifestyles. We don't want to stop living on chocolate chips and Red Bull. We want results with as little effort or change in our lifestyle as possible. Bottom line: you can take as many pills as you want, but if you don't change your lifestyle, you won't change your weight.

Diet supplements can also put you on an emotional roller coaster ride of try/fail, try/fail. That's not healthy either.

Listen, I need to stop here, but I could go on and on. Instead, I will put it on my list to write a Dirt book about this stuff. Deal?

steroids

tobacco

Tobac

Before we inhale too deeply in the tobacco zone, let's get one argument out of the way: Marketing works! It works on me. It works on you. Yeah, we all sit around and tell each other, "Oh, it doesn't work on me." If you truly believe that, then you are the perfect target, 'cause you are oblivious to the fact that it's working on you. Why do you think Nike pays $90 million to some dude just for wearing a pair of shoes on camera? Because he can make shoes better than anyone else? Uh, no, it's marketing. Cool athlete wears the tires and we buy them. They don't make you run faster, jump higher, or play better—it's a freakin' shoe! No, it's all about the cabbage, the duckies, the dollars.

Now, let's take a quick peek at cigarette companies. You think your job scrubbing out portable toilets after the county fair was tough, try this. Cigarette companies have a product

CO

that turns your teeth yellow, makes your breath stink, takes away thousands of your dollars, makes you all leathery and wrinkly, and kills you, and they have to convince people they need it.

Go back to the shoes. It would be like if those high-dollar shoes made your feet stink. Plus, every time you wore them, they took your money and made you look old and crusty. And the more you wore them, the more your legs became infected, until your legs had to be amputated. Crazy tough job to sell shoes that way.

So what were the cig companies' tactics to get past the nasty truth? Ignore it. That's it. Just pretend it's not really that way. Then they capped their brilliance by getting cigs into the hands of really hot, sexy, powerful people and hoping the general public (that would be us) would be big enough morons not to figure it out.

Changing Channels

Here's something I don't understand. People who have smoked their whole life go to the doc, the doc tells them they have cancer, and they're totally shocked. C'mon, you gotta be joking. Why are they so blown away? What did they expect to happen? Shaa!

Okay, we could go into all the cig facts that you already know, like all the poisonous stuff in cigarette smoke, and that over 1,000 people per day die from smoking-related stuff, and that it could cause all kinds of cancers, heart problems, and dying an early and nasty death. But talking about all that stuff would bore me till my head exploded, and if you don't know that stuff by now, there's nothing I can do for you. So we're moving on.

Let's talk about a very important issue: SEX.

Great, now that I've got your attention, I'm talking about being hot and hooking up with hotness.

Question: What's hot? When you run the pic of babeness in your head, what does it look like? His eyes? Her hair? His smile? Her smell? How do they feel? How do they taste when you kiss 'em? Yum-dillie-yum!

Oh, and what kind of stuff do you guys do together? Picnics? Roller coasters? Biking? Playing ball? Shopping? Reading? Anything you want? What do you imagine in your mentals that you guys do when you're just livin' life?

Yeah, baby! Perfect stuff. Now do a little retro-flash and remember that your life is more than just this moment. It's about so much more. You remember the deal—where are you at on the lifeline? Yeah, g'head and mark it again.

Born   83

Now let's play a little fortune-telling game. Let's just say that you tried smoking today. It made you feel better, even older, and way cool, so you keep on doing it. You live your life and you find the hotness of love that you always dreamed of— it's the person you had in your brain 2 paragraphs above this one. They're perfect. Oh yeah, and they smoke too, 'cause usually

[Notice from our legal counsel: We must remind you that any reference to sex is done under the assumption of marriage first. If you are confused about the order of events, please refer to The Dirt on Sex.]

smokers attract smokers. And you will be together in the fairy tale happily ever after.

Now that you got your little lifetime love, we will go back to our previously scheduled discussion on sex. To get there from here, let's take a quick little peek-a-boo at a study from the Andrology Institute of America. They studied all the sex issues of couples who smoked and couples who didn't. Well, get this, Mr. Smoking-Makes-Me-Sexy: the results showed that smokers had half the sex non-smokers did. Did you catch that? Non-smokers had twice as much sex as the smokers. And non-smokers enjoyed it more. On a scale of 0 to 10 with 10 being "extremely satisfactory," non-smokers said their sex life was an 8.7. Smoking couples had a weak 5.2 rating.

So fellas, girls, people, you wanna have a super-charged sex life? Then give up the sex killers. (And refer back to the Legal Notice.)

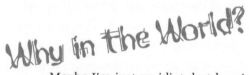

Why in the World?

Maybe I'm just an idiot, but here's my question: with all this Freddy Krueger type of horrible stuff connected to cigs, why do people start?

TOO YOUNG AND TOO OLD

The first answer to always pop up is to look older. Okay, don't go ask the young and the stupid if they started smoking to look older, 'cause you probably won't get that answer. People don't just wake up and have this little schizophrenic convo in their head about smoking and conclude, "I want to appear to be more mature than my chronological age displays." Naw, man, it's more of a vibe thing. Smoking is an "adult" thing. Ya know, it's not for kids. So it's kinda just an automatic connection that if you wanna appear older, then you smoke, 'cause it's for adults only.

It's so not true. Check it. If you look like a young kid so you smoke to look older, you don't look older. Nopers. You just look like a young kid smoking. You look stupid.

Now don't get me wrong, *eventually* you *will* look older, but it will be when you wanna look younger. By then it's too late. You'll already be the hot young babe with the grayish leathery skin, wrinkles around your lips and eyes, yellow teeth, bad breath, and dark circles under your eyes. Hmmm. The poster child of attractiveness.

The average smoker spends about $2,400 per year on cigarettes. Let's play a little numbers game. Let's say you only smoke for 20 years. Do the math. That means that you would blow $48,000 on the very thing that would kill you.

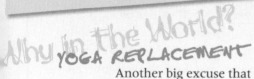

Why in the World?

YOGA REPLACEMENT

Another big excuse that people give for doing the Smokey the Bear impression is to relax. Well, I guess it depends on what your definition of relax is. 'Cause when you smoke, your body does a lot of things, but relaxing isn't one of them. In fact, your blood pressure goes up because smoking constricts the blood vessels, which keeps the blood from flowing like it's supposed to. This in turn makes the heart work harder. Nothing here is relaxing.

Okay, here's my take on the whole relaxation thing. To smoke a cig, you inhale these deep breaths to get the stuff into your lungs. You take about 10 or 15 minutes to smoke it down. Here's a thought: next time you feel the need to relax and whip out a cig, just take a 10-minute break and take a bunch of deep breaths. I know that probably sounds way stupid to you. But I guarantee it will make you feel relaxed, and it doesn't sound nearly as stupid as putting a bunch of dried leaves in your mouth, lighting them on fire, sucking down the result, and calling it relaxing.

Why in the World?
THE NICO-DIET

Smoking to control weight—this one is more of a girl issue, but it's becoming a guy thing too. In a weird way, people convince themselves that if they have something else going on with their hands, they won't eat as much. Try knitting! Whatever the excuse, the real issues are self-control and health issues. You trade one addiction for the other and one way of trashing your body for another.

In 1985 the term "smoker's face" was added to the medical dictionary.

It was
determined
that you
could
identify
people

who had smoked 10 or more years
by their facial features.

Friend Check

Do a quick friend check. Do your buds smoke? If so, that's a monster check engine light that you will smoke too. I know, you're your own person, you make your own decisions, la-ti-da. But you end up talking, looking, and doing the things your closest pals do. That's why you're best buds. If they play ball, you probably do too. Or at least you are a fan. There's some kind of connection there. If they go to church, you probably do too. So if they smoke, then you probably will too. It's just the way it flows.

So let's do a little *what if* kinda thing. Let's say you start smoking—hey, odds are some of you reading this have already gotten into the stuff. Grab a pen and do a little follow the leader on what you read next.

According to the group Action on Smoking and Health, a 30-year-old smoker can expect to live about 35 more years. Check it. A 30-year-old *non*-smoker can expect to live 53 more years.

> Every cigarette a person smokes
> reduces his life by 11 minutes.
> Each carton of cigarettes
> is a day and a half of lost life.
> Every year a person smokes
> shortens his life by almost 2 months.
> —University of California,
> Berkeley Wellness Letter

○ Put your mark on the line for how old you are right now.

○ Think about when you started smoking for the first time, or when you think you might. Even if you could never see yourself sucking on the nasty stuff, still put a mark down to answer the Q of "If I ever did start, when would it probably be?" (It would almost definitely be before you were 20.) Just play along here.

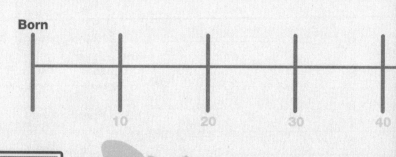

Now we are going to map out the beautiful consequences of the smoking vibe. Think in the futuristic and scratch this stuff on the line.

◯ Mark where you notice you start coughing a lot and even hacking up phlegm.

◯ Put your scribble on the age when you stop playing sports because it's too hard to breathe.

◯ X where you will find out you have lung cancer from the smoking.

◯ Oh, and here's a little trick. Take the last age—ya know, the age when you will die—and move that X up 25 years, 'cause smokers generally jump on the death wagon 25 years earlier. (Oh yeah, so that probably means all the other stuff is moved forward a few ticks on your yearly calendar too.)

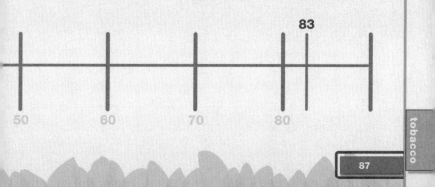

83

50   60   70   80

> Smoking 1 pack of cigarettes takes 28 minutes away from your life. A typical smoker loses 25 years of life expectancy.
>
> —*Dying to Quit*, Janet Bringham

Okay, I can't just leave you hanging here with a downer death vibe. So here's the deal. Go back to your dreams. All those things that you really want to do. These are things that can be enjoyed even more without the smokescreen. Don't buy the lies and, even bigger, **don't lie to yourself about what smoking will do for you**. It's a con job and you are the target.

Hey! What's with
the yellow haze?

What's
wrong with
it? I think it
makes me
look older.

Warning: The Designer General has determined that smoking
makes everything about you, including your lungs,
a very unappealing color.

tobacco

89

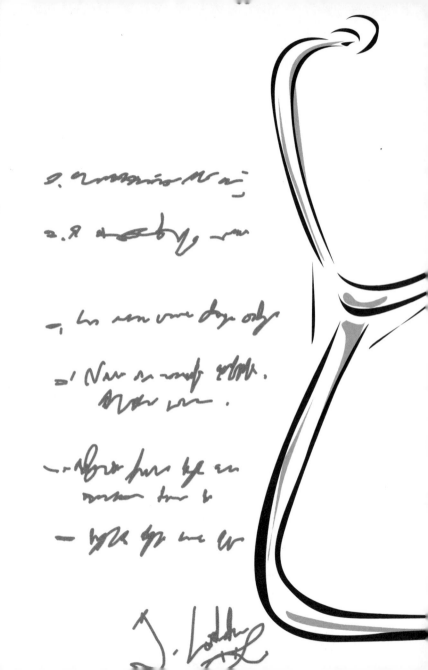

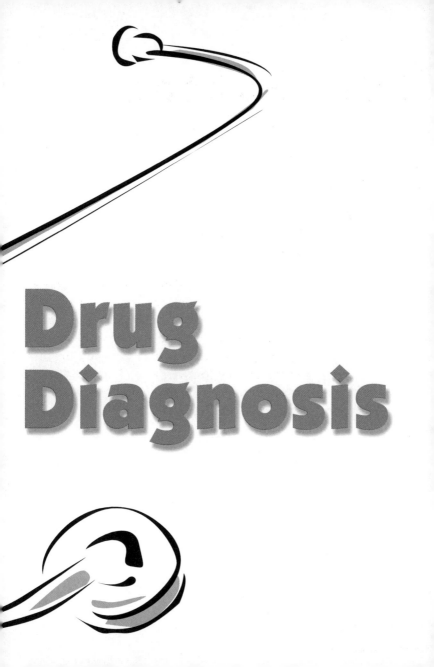

Drug
Diagnosis

The Y Factor

The big question of this whole book is *Why?* There has to be a reason why people do drugs. Well, duh. Of course there is. Actually, there are several reasons. And when any of these reasons start outweighing all the stupid effects that we know about, that's when people start getting into the stuff. Let's look at the biggies.

Cool Factor

Nobody likes to be the odd man out. I mean, my feelings get hurt if I'm the only one not invited to go out to eat. So I know it's really tough when you're at a pal's house and everyone starts drinking or something. Usually one person starts it, then their best little mini-me jumps in and does it, and before you know it there are a bunch of people who didn't want to do it, well, doing it. And there you are, sticking out. Everyone looking at you like you just walked outta the restroom and forgot to pull your pants up. You gotta stick with what you know, not what you feel. It's not cool to trash your body, to blow your future. It's definitely not cool to do something just because you don't want to be left out. Hey, if they are doing loser things, that means you got left out of being a loser.

And then you have the media cool factor. Oh, sure, you have all these people standing up saying drugs are bad—as they are being driven to the rehab clinic. Why do you think MJ started making a comeback? It's not because it's new or that the negatives no longer exist. I think it's because MJ is all over the movies, videos, music, and anywhere else they can feed you their agenda. Just because someone says it's cool, other people believe it must be true. Uh . . . nope.

Sooo Bored

I hate being bored. Man, just sitting around doing nothing . . . yuckness. And you know, I have thought about doing some really stupid things just because I was bored. But listen, when you hit the dull zone, that's when it's time to get moving. Change what you're doing. If you ever say, "There's nothing to do," then you're not looking. There is always something to do. Go outside. Read. Go for a walk. Practice throwing playing cards across the room like a ninja. Anything. Life is full of little things and biggies. You don't have to sit around and be bored.

Great Escape

Some people are just trying to get out of their life. They are looking for an escape from reality, so they get into anything they think will take them away. Well, the trouble is, you aren't gone. That would be like saying you wanna escape from prison so you're gonna get high. Dude, you didn't get outta prison. You're still in the same place. You're still gonna have to deal with life. So deal. You wanna escape, then escape. I mean, escape for real. Figure out what is the quickest way and will give you the most power to get out. Hey, if you are in high school with a crappy home life, then the quickest, most powerful way to get out may be for you to pour yourself into your education so you can graduate with a scholarship to college so you can get outta where you are.

All Grown Up

So many teens get into stuff, especially alcohol and to-bacco, because they are adult things. If you do them, you must be an adult, right? No, you're a stupid-looking kid. And as for the drug side, if you do that to look like an adult, well, adults who do drugs are lawbreaking idiots. So if you did accomplish looking like an adult, you'd look like a grown–up, criminal idiot. Congrats.

I'm My Own
BOSS

Many teens get into these things because they want to prove they are independent and can make their own decisions. And some do it just to totally rebel. Well, I don't think it's working like you think it should. I mean, yeah, if your definition of rebellion is to drive your life right into the ground just to prove you can, well, great, I have faith in you. But hey, if you really want to shock the parentals, bring home all As. That will blow their minds. If you want to prove that you can do anything you want and you don't need them, then do the unexpected—come home 15 minutes before you are supposed to be home. Man, there are so many ways to mess with people's heads by shocking them AND throwing a totally positive vibe into your life.

Why Not?

Hey, I love to try new things. It's in me. My motto is **"Live with no regrets."** And I follow that up with the belief that until God is finished with me, I am invincible. Now, that is balanced out with an understanding of the rule, "Do not put the LORD

your God to the test." So that means, skydiving . . . I'm in.
Skydiving without a parachute

.

.

.

                                I'm out.
That also means I will try any food you put in front of me.
I will put it in my body to see if I like it. But I will not put
chemicals in my body that I know could have a short-term
feel-good effect and a lot of negatives. I don't want anything faking the way I feel. I want to experience life raw
and feel what it really is like. So experiment. Try new
things. But there are so many ways to do that, so
many things to try that will explode your life in
a good way, that you don't need to mess with
stuff that will mess with you. So go do it.
Live without regrets.

Drugs and You

The pressure is on. You know that you will be hit with at least 1 of these issues, and many of you are in the battle right now. You want to make the right decision, but it's hard. Trust me, I know how hard it can be. If you're going to swim through the crazy waters of your teen years without drowning in some drug, you first gotta know what kind of person you are. Once you've got that figured out, then you can get your game plan together on how you are going to breeze past the battle zones. Which one of these sounds like you?

To achieve the full design effect of this page, align the top of this page with the top of your neckline while holding it with the words facing out. Stand this way in front of a mirror. Please make sure to color the collar to match whatever outfit you are wearing.

The Follower

It is totally okay to be a follower. For the most part we all are. Hey, there can only be one guy standing at the front of the line; everyone else is a follower. But this can get you in some danger zones quick if you don't keep an eye on who you are following and where you are going. So when you find yourself in a bad place, you got a couple of options.

1. This may be the time you take a stand. You may find a new confidence in yourself when you decide to totally skip out on a party where you know there will be some uncool stuff happening. If you really wanna test your confidence level, don't just turn down the invite but speak up and tell 'em why.

2. Keep doing what you normally do—follow. But change the person you are following. If the crowd you're hanging with is starting on a bad ride, switch buses and follow a different crowd.

The Curious

You still have that childlike curiosity. You love to explore, to ask questions. Thomas Edison was one of you. (Thanks for the lightbulb, Tommy.) The Curious always ask *Who? What? When? Where? Why? How?* and all the other questions to figure out why things work the way they do and if there is a better way. Curiosity is a gift. But have you heard the saying "curiosity killed the cat"? Don't know what that means? Then go look on some highways and it will start making sense. Sad, I know. But true. See, the curiosity is what gets a lot of your group in trouble. You want to know about things on your own. You want to see if what everyone says is true. Listen, keep the curiosity. Keep asking questions. But learn from the experiences of others. That's what the great curious people did. With alcohol and drugs, check out the long-terms of using by studying other people's mistakes. That will give you time and energy to focus on the whole world of stuff that's there for you to explore.

The Leader

You take charge. You make a decision and take a stand. And sometimes that's what gets you in trouble. When you won't start smoking or boozing or drugging, people who are doing it might question you and think you're being a wuss. Take a stand and prove them wrong. Listen, being a leader means you gotta be going somewhere. You have people following you, and they will go where you go. If you start doing stupid things, they will too. So be a leader and walk away. You'll feel stronger for it, and a bunch of people behind you will be letting out a sigh of relief because they didn't want to do it either.

The Adventurer

Life is a rush. You like to push it to the extreme. If there is something new, different, untried, you're in. This is where many of your compadres crash. They get it in their mentals that drugs, alcohol, or tobacco is some wild adventure to ride. And I suppose it sorta is. But real adventure comes from not knowing your outcome. And we just covered all the outcomes you can expect with drugs. Not much of a surprise left. Which means not a whole lot of real adventure there. So live life as a *true* adventure. When someone tries to throw your vibe off with drugs and stuff, just remember, you don't need it. Live adventurously and you'll do stuff sober that most people are too scared to do even on drugs. So live!

Still need more convincing that drugs are a wacked-out way to go? Well, I've got some more ammo for you. But what makes sense to you is going to depend on what kind of person you are. Check it out.

Health Conscious: Know that any time you throw chemicals into your body's prepackaged recipe, you are trashing the process and hurting your body. Even the stuff that seems to be used to make you healthier, like steroids or diet pills, is hurting the body's systems. The experts even tell us to be careful with weak meds like aspirin 'cause it could eat holes in your stomach. The body was made to function in a very specific way. If you are really into health and your body, then do a little studying on the body systems and start looking for natural methods like foods, exercise, or natural supplements to help your body function the way you want it to without adding chemicals.

Social Activist: Many socially minded people are all about social freedom and allowing everyone to make their own choices about what they do with their lives. Well, look, if you are a socially minded person and you are questioning what the big fuss is over drugs, alcohol, or tobacco, then go hang out at a children's hospital and work with the kids who are seriously messed up for life because their parents were on drugs. Attend the family funeral of someone who died in a head-on collision with a drunk driver. Even better, sit as close as possible to the one person who survived. If you are a social justice kind of person, you will realize that doing drugs is not exercising your freedom. It's allowing a 5-year-old girl to be raped by a drug dealer so her mom can get another fix. It's paying for the assassination of a judge's family because he put a drug lord in jail. If you consider the whole world your friend, remember that people who use the drugs, alcohol, and tobacco are allowing thousands of your friends to die, get messed up, commit suicide, or just to drop out of life.

Listen, it's a supply and demand issue. If no one bought the stuff, there would be no need for the stuff. If there was no need for the stuff, there'd be no production. No production, no problem. Don't be part of the demand problem.

Financial Wizard: You will quickly start adding up the coin. It doesn't matter what kind of drug you choose to get into; it will cost you lots of cash. Even if you don't do it yourself, just tolerating drugs is costing you big time. Tobacco-related illnesses are costing you big money even if you don't smoke. Alcohol, drugs, it's all costing you. Who do you think pays the bills when someone has to go to the ER on a drug overdose and they don't have the money to pay? You do! Who pays the hospital bills when someone who can't pay dies because of tobacco? You do! Yeah, if you throw your money away on the stuff you are just setting it on fire and watching it burn. But it also takes a big chunk outta your pocket if you just let it keep hooking other people.

Goal Oriented: The drugs and other substances can totally rob you of your future. They take over your life. They become your life. Yeah, hard drugs grab you and rip you apart quickly. But even marijuana gets you. Yeah, it makes you mellow—so mellow that many people don't even care about goals anymore. They just wanna smoke dope. Tobacco—it becomes your constant companion. You drive with it. Eat with it. Dance with it. You go to sleep with it. You wake up with it. If you're someone who really wants to design your life and make it happen, life has no room for drugs, alcohol, or tobacco.

Religious Person: Here's a question: Would you go out, break into a church or a temple of some sort, and just start trashing the place? Spray paint the walls, break the windows, burn the Bibles? Probably not. Well, the Holy

Bible says that the body is the temple of God. Yeah, your body. And trashing it is exactly what is happening when someone uses any of the stuff we are talking about in this book (and a lot of stuff that's not here too). And there's a reason it's called getting wasted—because it's wasting your time, your body, and the experience of life that the Creator has given you.

People get into these negative things because they have a void of some sort in their lives. They don't like their life. Or they don't like their body. They don't think they are accepted by other people. Whatever. Hey, sometimes God allows those voids for a reason—so that we have to search for something to fill that void, and that something is him. But when people throw some chemical in the void, they totally miss out on God.

One more little tidbit and I'll let you move on. The Bible says that no one can serve 2 masters.* Check it. Anything that has control of you is your master. If you are addicted to anything, it controls you. If it's, let's say, cigarettes, then they are your master. No one can serve 2 masters. Think about it.

* Read it for yourself in the book of Matthew, chapter 6, verse 24.

We're about done with all the drug stuff, but I just can't walk away without spouting off some thoughts on how to make keeping away from the junk a little easier. Before you read this, though, you gotta know that this isn't a formula to overcome addiction or heavy drug issues. If any of this stuff has affected your life, crashed your grades, trashed your relationships with friends or fam, you need to get to a counselor or someone who can help you through this. It will be tough, but you can do it.

Those of you who are just toying with the idea of doing tobacco or any of the other drugs, humor me for a sec. Quit planning when you might try it or trying to figure out if it is really that bad for you or not. Here's what I want you to do: think about whatever it is you are thinking about getting into. Alcohol? Marijuana? Smoking? Whatever it is that is throwing you pop-ups in your mind. Now ask yourself and answer yourself this **Q: "Why do I want to do_____?"** (Fill in the blank with whatever you are thinking about.) Think about all the reasons. You will definitely start by giving yourself some really lame answers like "I want to because I want to and I make my own decisions and no one else influences them." But keep asking yourself to go deeper. Keep saying, "No, really, why do I want to do this?" Be real with yourself and you will get the real answer. Most of the time there is an acceptance issue or a pain issue or something else that is leading you toward some bad roads.

When you get to the real issue, start working on that. If yours is the fact that you think no one will like you, then it's a self-esteem and acceptance issue. Figure out what you can do to start feeling better about you. It may be working out or hooking up with a hyper youth group. But work on the real issues, 'cause chemicals won't fix the prob.

Be smart here. If you've never been asked to do any of this stuff, you can bet you will. You gotta have a plan before you get thrown in the game. You first have to decide that you are going to say no. If you haven't made that decision yet, then you're probably going down. Be solid on that choice, and then the natural next question is, "How?"

Here are a few of my faves to use when people ask me if I want drugs, tobacco, or alcohol. There are so many ways to do it, so find ones that work for you and stick with them. Some of them are fun, and some of them may seem to be rude . . . and they are. I don't really care, though, 'cause don't you think it's pretty rude

You first have to decide that you are going to say no.

for someone to try to get you to do something that you really don't want to do or that could really mess up your life? Here ya go:

1. "Naw, that's not my vibe."

2. "Nope, but thanks for asking. Bu-bye."

3. "No, thank you, drive through!"

4. "No. Would you like that supersized?"

5. "Huh?" Say it as if you didn't hear them. And when they repeat it, just keep going "Huh? Huh?" Count how many times it takes them to go away.

6. "Oh, look at the time. Sorry, you have to go now."

7. "I think I hear your mommy calling you."

8. "Oh, wow, and be like you? Nope!"

9. "No, I'm allergic to it."

10. Throw your hands up in the air like a little kid and shout, "Stranger Danger!"

11. "Moooo! That's cow for 'Go away.'"

12. "No way. There are supposed to be undercover police here tonight. . . . You might be one of them." (Do this convincingly and they will weird out for the rest of the night.)

13. Just stare at them and say absolutely nothing. This is way fun.

Remember that it may be a close friend who asks you to do this stuff. They may think they are being friendly, or including you, or, I don't know, something else. Sometimes you just have to get in their face. I remember spending the day with a friend and he probably asked me 15 times if I wanted a drink. I didn't, so I just said "No thanks" every time. Finally, after asking me 3 times within like 90 seconds, I just shouted, "No! I don't want anything to drink, and don't ask me again!" I did this way loud so other people could hear me. He was embarrassed, he apologized, and he didn't ask me again.

Real quick let me throw at you some important stuff on how to keep yourself from getting sucked into the toilet of drugs. Here are a few little hints to make life a little easier. You gotta make a plan. If you don't think about it ahead of time, you will get blindsided, and you may crumble.

1. Check out the sitch. If you know there's going to be some bad stuff happening, then throw out another plan and sell it to your buds. Lots of times if there are other options, your friends will take the out.

2. Know what you are going to say before someone offers you something. Pick a couple of your favorite lines and use 'em.

3. **Have an out.** When you are going somewhere you're not too sure about, have a way out in advance.

4. **Buddy up.** Don't just hang alone. Keep a pal close to you who is not into the drugs, alcohol, or tobacco scene. There is strength in numbers.

This stuff isn't genius. It's simple and it's real. If you want to survive, you have to have a plan, and you have to be strong enough to deal with your issues and not try to cover them up or find acceptance by using any of these chemicals. And you have to know why *and* how to say no.

The Dirt is Done

So there it is. *The Dirt on Drugs*. Not a total encyclopedia of everything there is to know. And definitely not all the info needed to face addiction. That needs to go to a counselor for major battle plans.

But I hope by now you have enough info on the effects and the consequences of some common drugs to make some serious decisions about what you want to do with your life. And hey, it *is* your life. Live it to the max. Protect it to the fullest. And live with no regrets.

Justin Lookadoo—the name says it all. He's a freak, let's just be frank. But even freaks can have a point, and Justin's is sharp enough to cut your heart out and serve it to you on a platter. He has an amazing ability to take simple truth and make you say, "Duh, why didn't I think of that?" And with this simple truth he'll turn your world upside down.

Justin has been doing this kind of stuff from stages for the past 12 years, yes, since he was just a pup. He was a juvenile probation officer for 5 years in the toughest part of East Texas. And just a few years ago he left the jail business to tour the U.S., speaking in public schools and at leadership conferences like MADD, DARE, and FFA. He speaks all over the country, so if you want him in your school or church, check out his web site for more info. Hopefully some day you'll get to see the tall one in person and allow him to Lookadoo ya.

In the meantime, check out one of his many books out there. He wrote *Step Off, The Hardest 30 Days of Your Life*. And boy, is it. Don't try this one unless you are prepared to work your butt off in the wildest adventure you've ever had. He also wrote a book called *Dateable* that will give you all kinds of great advice about dating and relationships. Check it out and look for all the other great Dateable books shown on the next page.

Dateable:
are you?
are they?

Justin Lookadoo and Hayley DiMarco

the
dateable
a guide to the sexes
rules

Justin Lookadoo and Hayley Morgan DiMarco

Don't
Miss
These

A Dateable Book

The *Dirt* on
Breaking Up

Hayley DiMarco & Justin Lookadoo

A Dateable Book

The *Dirt* on
Sex

Justin Lookadoo

A Datea

The *Dirt* on
Dating

Hayley DiMarco